Mindfulness

Overcoming the Power of Fear and Anxiety

Aaron Kelly

Sermon To Book
www.sermontobook.com

Mindfulness / Aaron Kelly
ISBN-13: 978-1-945793-24-0
ISBN-10: 1-945793-24-4

To the Fresh Church Launch Team. May you soar through life with your heads held high. You are amazing, and I cherish each one of you. Thank you for aligning yourself with the vision God gave Jacqui and me. This book is because of you.
–Ps. Aaron

To my children, Chris & Judah. You have been born into a challenging era. One of deep of uncertainty, anxiety, and fear. My prayer for both of you is that you always know that God is fighting for you and there is no problem so large that it should cause you to retreat from life in fear. Take every thought captive and make it obedient to Jesus, and always keep your eyes on Him. Praise Him in every season and take hold of all that He has for you.
–Dad

To my wife, Jacqui. Thank you for always cheering me on and drawing God's greatness out of me. You inspire me to keep striving for more of the Kingdom of God. I love you and look forward to many more days of building the Kingdom of God with you.
–Aaron.

CONTENTS

The Age of Disconnect

When you're sitting in a restaurant, surrounded by family or friends, how often do you check your smartphone?

This habit is becoming all too common in this present-day society and is revealing the ever apparent truth that we are extremely disconnected people, who in turn are struggling with the overwhelming issue of fear and anxiety.

The famous evangelist Billy Graham said, "Historians will probably call our era 'the age of anxiety.'"[1] You've got the Stone Age, you've got the Ice Age, and then you've got our era, the age of anxiety. What a way to be remembered!

Our anxiety stems ultimately from our disconnection—our social alienation from each other as well as our spiritual alienation from God. Preferring electronic communication over face-to-face communication is simply one of the most obvious manifestations of our disengagement from the relationships that matter most.

I've been in ministry for over a decade, and many people have approached me for help and guidance on the challenges they're facing in their lives. More often than not, I've found that when we strip the surface layers from our problems, we find fear or anxiety lurking at the bottom. I've held countless conversations, counselling situations, and prayer sessions for people who are struggling with stressful circumstances and deep-seated anxiety.

Anxiety is the bane of our generation, and while human invented measures like therapy and adult colouring books can provide a certain amount of relief, they don't address the root of the problem.

Most of us enjoy great material blessing, often taking our basic needs for granted, and this tempts us to believe in our self-sufficiency. We no longer rely on God in the way past generations have relied on and been keenly aware of His providence.

Because we aren't as aware of our continuous need for God—the One who supplies everything—we don't learn to lean on Him. Yet our human insufficiencies undermine our claims of self-sufficiency, and thus anxiety claims us.

However, anxiety is contrary to God's plan for us. He doesn't want us to be anxious! And we don't need to be.

And That's an Order!

Second Timothy 1:7 clearly instructs us, "For God has not given us a spirit of fear and timidity" (NLT). Fear and anxiety were never His intention for us.

When He knit you together—when He formed you, before your mum and dad even imagined your existence—He designed you to be filled with power, love, and self-control. Somewhere along the way however, we let fear and anxiety creep in. We focus on our problems, needs, and dangers, instead of on God's ability to provide.

That's not God's best for us.

God doesn't want you to be anxious *at all*. Paul wrote in Philippians 4:6: "...do not be anxious about anything." This is a command—it's not as if God's Word says, "I think you should probably not be anxious." He doesn't advise, "It's highly recommended you refrain from being anxious, because it doesn't feel good."

Instead, what He is saying is, "Don't allow anxiety to have a foothold in your life."

Easier said than done, right? I know every single person, Christian or non-Christian, will battle with anxiety and fear. We all battle with the lies of the enemy as they come against us.

When everything seems to be going wrong, we must learn to develop and maintain skills that fill our minds with the right thoughts. In short, this entails focussing on God, relying on Him, and praising His goodness.

And as we'll see in chapter 3, we can praise God anytime, anywhere. Unlike our smartphones, praising and worshiping God doesn't rely on a good Wi-Fi connection or battery power. Praise is not a matter of having a worship leader, a stage, or even a band.

Rather, it's about lifting up God's name in your heart—and letting His Spirit fill you and your praise.

In this book, as we learn more about the power of renewing our mind to dispel anxiety, we will turn repeatedly to the biblical narrative of King Jehoshaphat, in 2 Chronicles chapter 20. This ancient king of Judah practiced four key principles that helped him to overcome the anxiety and fear he faced:

1. Trap your thoughts.
2. Turn your head.
3. Train your tongue.
4. Take your victory!

If we could take these same four principles and apply them when anxiety rears its head in our lives, then we too will be strengthened to overcome the fear and anxiety we so often encounter.

Therefore, accompanying each main chapter of this book you will find a workbook section. The workbook includes reflection questions and an application-oriented action statement to help you begin integrating these key principles into your daily spiritual life.

If we, as God's people, can understand the origins of fear, anxiety, and our relational disconnect, and learn to practice these mindfulness techniques in our daily lives, then the only one filled with anxiety will be the enemy!

As we close the distance between our habits of mind and God's design for us, and renew our commitment to our relationships with God and others, we will think twice before texting someone sitting right across the table from us. As we realise more fully that the truth of God's Word trumps the lies and fears our spiritual enemy deals out, we will step forward into a new season of victory, strength, and power.

CHAPTER ONE

The Origins of Fear and Anxiety

Long before anxiety and fear were ever something you experienced, you were given a gift far greater. Second Timothy 1:6–7 says, "For this reason I remind you to fan into flame the gift of God, which is in you through the laying on of my hands, for God gave us a spirit not of fear but of power and love and self-control."

This gift, offered to you by God, is one that is designed to combat the fear and anxiety the enemy tries to give you through little events every day. It will ensure you live an abundant and victorious life if you accept it, embrace it, and use it. It is the gift of the Holy Spirit.

The members of my family love giving and receiving gifts. In fact, we love it so much that we often can't wait until the special day to give our loved ones the gift we've purchased for them. In the days leading up to birthdays and Christmas, we drop hints and tempt the other person until eventually we decide, "You may as well just open it now!"

Imagine our disappointment if the recipient chose not to receive the gift. If we knew the gift would be something they would love and benefit from, we would do everything we could to encourage them to open and use it. We would try to explain all it can be used for, and we would demonstrate how great the gift is. But ultimately, the choice of accepting and using that gift would be their decision.

This is the same with God's gift of the Holy Spirit. Luke 11:13 says, "If you then, though you are evil, know how to give good gifts to your children, how much more will your Father in heaven give the Holy Spirit to those who ask Him!" (NIV). The gift of the Holy Spirit is better than any gift we could ever imagine, and God is ready to give it to those who ask Him.

When you decide to follow Jesus and believe He is Lord, you immediately receive this gift. The day you "believed, you were marked in him with a seal, the promised Holy Spirit, who is a deposit guaranteeing our inheritance..." (Ephesians 1:13–14 NIV). This deposit of the Holy Spirit into your soul is the very thing that secures your salvation, for which Jesus paid, and ensures your eternity with Him. In addition, the Holy Spirit in us is the power, love, and self-control we need to overcome fear and anxiety daily.

Desired by the Father, Paid for By the Son, Guaranteed by the Spirit

The dwelling of the Holy Spirit in our lives became available because of Jesus. He came to give us life in abundance, here and now and for eternity. The only way He could do so was to die for all humanity and, in turn, leave us with the Holy Spirit, who is the promise of His presence in our everyday lives. God desires that we encounter His transforming power through a relationship with Him—but many have not.

It is with this knowledge in mind that we look at the origins of fear and our relationship with God. This is the most important aspect of overcoming fear and anxiety.

The four practical keys given in this book will be effective in finding freedom for our minds. And they are most powerful when we find freedom from sin in Jesus first and receive His salvation. If you understand His love for you, then "confess with your mouth that Jesus is Lord and believe in your heart that God raised Him from the dead, you will be saved" (Romans 10:9). This means you will receive the love of Jesus and take the first steps in finding eternal freedom from fear and anxiety.

In the beginning, God created male and female for a relationship with Him and each other. The first humans walked through life knowing complete unity with God. In their home, the Garden of Eden, there was no pain or suffering, no lack or poverty, no hatred or violence. Everything that's wrong with our world today did not exist. There was complete freedom and harmony in this utopia.

The first humans, Adam and Eve, were given rule and authority over every living thing (Genesis 1:26). They walked daily with God. They had an overflowing amount of food from every tree in the garden, except for one tree—the tree of the knowledge of good and evil (Genesis 2:16). If they ate from this tree, they would die (Genesis 2:17).

God set this one rule in place to protect the hearts of Adam and Eve. The rule wasn't designed to take away pleasure or to stop them from enjoying all they had. Rather, it was set to ensure they could enjoy it all without being overcome by knowledge greater than they could handle, which would ultimately result in fear, anxiety, guilt, and shame.

Unfortunately, the enemy, Satan, jealous of this united relationship between humanity and God, desired to break it down. He knew that the way he could destroy this perfect unity was to bring imperfection into the world. If sin (doing the opposite of what God desires) entered the hearts of humankind, it would sever the relationship they had with God—in which case, the enemy thought, he would win.

Satan appeared to Eve in Genesis 3 and convinced her to try the fruit from the one tree she knew was off limits. Satan did this by using the trick he still uses today to spark fear in our minds: the lie. The moment she and Adam bought into the lie and ate this fruit, they were filled with the measurable results of sin—fear and shame—and suffered the consequence of sin, which was separation from God.

Adam and Eve's first response after sinning was to hide from God out of fear (Genesis 3:8), not because they had done the wrong thing but because they realized they were naked and were ashamed. Things that were once innocent, pure, and a sign of freedom had now become distorted and violated. Their thoughts started to become twisted with lies, sparking the first feelings of fear and anxiety.

God's original desire in creating humanity, including you and me, was that we would be in a perfect relationship with Him for eternity. This was destroyed for the rest of time by one choice to disobey Him. God explained that the full consequence of this disobedience would be death.

Before this, life was eternal. The world, Eden, was perfect. But once sin entered the picture, this perfect world and eternal life were no longer guaranteed.

Some may feel this is unjust, unloving, or ungracious. In truth, however, it is the purest form of love on display. God had every power to remove the tree or remove Eve's ability to take fruit from the tree, but He didn't— because He loved humanity.

His desire wasn't to create robots who would love Him or obey His rule as God because they had been programmed to do so. His desire was, and always will be, for people He has created in love to make their own choices.

He wants us to choose to love Him in return and to demonstrate this love by obeying Him. If He hadn't created us without this ability to choose, our love would not be true love.

Some may question the extreme consequence for eating one piece of fruit. Key to understanding our separation from God by sin is realizing that God is perfect. He is perfect in His love, in His holiness, in His actions, in His justice—in everything He does. A perfect

God, by His very nature, cannot be united with imperfection.

Throughout the Old Testament, from Adam onward, we see the consequence of sin being applied to people when their imperfection encountered God's perfection. When God's perfect presence was in the same place as the presence of sinful humanity, they would die. Sin resulted inevitably in physical death as well as an eternal spiritual death—that is, separation from God.

A Temporary Solution

God desired a relationship with people He loved in which they would be filled with life. In the book of Exodus, God asked Moses to "make a sanctuary for me, and I will dwell among them" (Exodus 25:8 NIV). This sanctuary, called the "tabernacle," was a holy and sacred place. It provided a temporary way for imperfect people to meet with their perfect God.

Its design was intricate in detail and beautiful in appearance. Every specification regarding its layout and the procedures to be completed before one could enter it were put in place to demonstrate God's desire for a relationship with His people.

Because they had been alienated from Him for quite some time, God needed to teach people how to relate to Him as a King who ruled, before they could enjoy freedom of relationship as Adam and Eve had known in the Garden of Eden—that is, anytime access to Him as a friend. The tabernacle was designed for people to be forgiven of their sins so they could inherit life once again.

The tabernacle was surrounded by a high fence with one gate as an entrance to the courtyard, which anyone could enter. Just inside the gate was a brazen altar, the place where a perfect male animal from a flock or herd would have to die to pay the price of death for sin.

The person bringing the animal would lay their hands on its head to identify with the sacrifice and to symbolize the movement of their sin from themselves to the creature. The high priest would then slaughter the animal and sprinkle its blood in front of the veil of the Holy Place. For as the New Testament makes clear, "The law requires that nearly everything be cleansed with blood, and without the shedding of blood there is no forgiveness." (Hebrews 9:22 NIV).

After the brazen altar, there was the laver, a large bronze bowl for the priest to wash his hands and feet before entering the tent. Doing so demonstrated that one must be clean before encountering God's presence.

The tent was split into two sections: first, the Holy Place, and second, the Holy of Holies. Inside the Holy Place was the menorah, the table of showbread, and the golden altar of incense.

The menorah was a lampstand, which was the only source of light in the Holy Place. Once the high priest lit the candles, it symbolized God's light invading the darkness of the human heart.

The table of showbread was a small wooden table where the high priest would put fresh bread weekly and eat it when performing his duties. This illustrated God's willingness to spend time with people. It was His invitation to communion and friendship with Him.

The golden altar of incense was placed in front of the curtain entrance to the Holy of Holies, the place where God's presence dwelt. The high priest would burn incense on this altar as a symbol of the prayers of God's people going up to Him like a sweet fragrance. God wanted them to know He enjoyed hearing their prayers. The high priest would then sprinkle this altar with the blood of the animal that was sacrificed outside to claim the forgiveness of their sin once again.

Behind this altar was the Holy of Holies. This small room was separated from the rest of the tent by a thick curtain, otherwise known as "the veil." This veil acted as a shield for imperfect and sinful humankind from the perfect presence of God. It was a barrier separating the world from God's presence.

Only the high priest was allowed to enter this place, once a year, on the Day of Atonement. He would do so with a rope around his ankle for people to pull him out again in case he had not cleansed himself sufficiently and was struck dead by the perfection of God's presence.

Inside the Holy of Holies was the ark of the covenant. This was the throne of God. The ark of the covenant was a box that concealed Aaron's staff, symbolizing God's power; a box of manna, symbolizing God's love through His provision; and the Ten Commandments, symbolizing God's desire for holy living and our self-control in obedience. If the high priest followed the process correctly, God's presence would come from the box like an uncontrollable light, and the high priest would encounter His presence.

The tabernacle was fine, for a temporary solution, because it offered people the chance to choose to be forgiven of their sin and in turn not die but have eternal life. However, the tabernacle did nothing in giving God the relationship He desired with everyone He had created.

The Permanent Fix

God's ultimate desire is that He could have a loving relationship with every person He has ever created. It is for this love "that He gave His only Son [Jesus], that whoever believes in Him should not perish but have eternal life" (John 3:16). Jesus fulfilled each part of that tabernacle so that we could have a relationship with Him.

Jesus told His followers He was:

The Gate (John 10:9)
The Perfect Lamb who was sacrificed for our sins (1 Peter 1:18–19)
The Laver who washes us clean (Ephesians 5:25-27)
The Light of the world (John 8:12)
The Bread of life (John 6:35)
The One who prays for us (Romans 8:34)

When Jesus died for you, He did so to pay the sin debt you owed. Jesus paid the ultimate price by shedding His blood on the cross. This is the ultimate sign of God's love for us—giving His only Son, Jesus, the only perfect

One, to die in our place. As Jesus was hanging on the cross, breathing His last breath, every sin ever committed or going to be committed filled His soul.

Can you imagine the pain of guilt something like this would cause? I know the gut-churning feeling I get when I do one thing wrong, but Jesus took the whole world's sin upon Himself at that moment. He became the perfect lamb sacrifice, once and for all.

Finally, He cried aloud "It is finished!" and exhaled for one last time (John 19:30). At that moment, the earth shook, the sky went black, and the curtain in the temple tore in two (Matthew 27:51).

This was a very significant moment for all of humanity! Because of Jesus taking our punishment of death, the perfect presence of God was no longer confined to the ark of the covenant, but was freely available to all. Humanity no longer needed the veil to shield them from the perfection of God. Sin's debt had been paid! God's people would now be seen by Him through the lens of His perfect Son, Jesus Christ.

It's interesting to note here an important link between the tabernacle and this moment. The ark of the covenant was the throne of God, which found its rule and would manifest His presence upon three things: power (Aaron's staff), love (manna), and the law requiring self-control (Ten Commandments). When Paul described to Timothy the gift of the Holy Spirit in 2 Timothy 1:6–7, he said that it is a Spirit of "power, love and self-discipline" (NIV). This gift that opposes fear in our lives is the same Spirit who would manifest in the tabernacle, the same Spirit who left the temple when the veil was torn, and the same Spirit who raised Jesus to life after being dead and buried.

Three days after dying on the cross and being buried, Jesus rose to life again, proving that He had conquered death once and for all. Everyone can now experience abundant life here on earth, inherit eternal life in heaven, and have a personal, loving relationship with God. It is through the resurrection power of Jesus, our relationship with Him, and being filled with His Spirit that we can shake off the grip of fear from our lives. The very same power that raised Jesus from the dead is now available to live in us by His Spirit.

First John 4:18 says, "There is no fear in love. But perfect love drives out fear…. The one who fears is not made perfect in love." (NIV). True and ultimate freedom from fear and anxiety comes from being made "perfect in love" through personally experiencing perfect love.

Every source of love we could ever chase in this world is imperfect. My love for my friends and family is imperfect because I am imperfect. I will inevitably let them down, do something that could hurt them, or fail them in some way because of that imperfection. The same is true for you. Perfect love can only come from someone who is perfect, and as we've seen, no human measures up to that standard.

The only source of perfect love is the love of Jesus, who gave His life for us and who desires to call us friends. John 15:13 says, "Greater love has no one than this, that he lay down his life for his friends." That's what Jesus did for you and me. This perfect love saves us from sin, death, and separation from God, and can ultimately set us free from fear and anxiety.

It does this by giving us access to the Holy Spirit, who makes our hearts His home and dwells within us upon our salvation. We can now become the tabernacle of God, housing His Spirit of power, love, and self-control.

This choice to make Jesus the Lord of your life and to encounter His perfect love, which will transform you, is the greatest choice you could ever make. You were created for a relationship with the God who created you. God desires that you find freedom from your sin and other baggage, like fear and anxiety, so that you can experience that relationship with Him.

All you need to do is believe in your heart that Jesus is Lord and declare that God raised Him from the dead. Put simply, believe He is now leading and directing your life—that He is God. Then you can live the life of an overcomer with the resurrection power of Jesus, the Holy Spirit, filling your soul and leading you in power, love, and self-discipline.

Below is a prayer I invite you to pray. Sincerely praying this prayer can be a powerful moment in your life—saving you through the perfect love of Jesus and giving you a fresh start in Him:

Dear Jesus,

Thank You for Your perfect love.

Thank You that You lived, died, and rose again so that I could have relationship with You, and have access to Your Spirit, which fills me with power, love, and self-discipline.

I'm sorry for living life my own way and not accepting the free gift of abundant and eternal life You have so freely given me.

Today I decide to follow You.

I invite You to fill me with Your Spirit and its resurrection power.

Fill me with power, love, and self-discipline.

I believe that You are Lord.

Help me to live for you every day of my life.

Amen.

If you prayed that prayer, congratulations! You have now been upgraded. Life will never be the same again if you choose daily to surrender it into the hands of Jesus and the power of His Spirit. I invite you to go to the following link and complete the short form there to let me know about your decision to follow Jesus and receive His power, love, and self-control:

https://www.aaronkelly.com.au/findlife

Now, I pray that God takes the rest of this book and helps you overcome the grip of fear and anxiety in your life!

Chapter 1 Questions

Question: How was life in the Garden of Eden different from life today?

_____

_____

_____

_____

_____

_____

_____

_____

_____

_____

_____

Question: When have you tried to give someone a gift they refused? How did that make you feel? How did you respond?

_____
_____
_____
_____
_____
_____
_____
_____
_____
_____
_____
_____

Question: What do you imagine daily life would be like if God didn't give you the ability to make your own choices? How would your relationship with God be different? What is the benefit of being able to choose between obedience and disobedience?

_____
_____
_____
_____
_____
_____
_____
_____
_____
_____

Question: When have you experienced disconnection from God? What does this alienation feel like? How did you—or how could you—reconnect with Him?

_____

_____

_____

_____

_____

_____

_____

_____

_____

_____

Question: How does the Spirit of God work against fear and anxiety?

_____

_____

_____

_____

_____

_____

_____

_____

_____

_____

Action: Thank God that He has given you the ability to choose Him! Surrender your sin and your sinfulness to Him by accepting the gift of His Son and His Spirit—and make Him the Lord of your daily life. Then embrace your new life with a spirit of power, love, and self-discipline, not of fear or anxiety.

Chapter 1 Notes

_____

_____

_____

_____

_____

_____

_____

_____

_____

_____

_____

_____

_____

_____

_____

_____

_____

_____

_____

_____

_____

_____

CHAPTER TWO

Trap Your Thoughts

Growing up, I was fairly certain my grandparents' house was haunted.

When I was in Grade 6, my parents sold their tiny house and we moved in with my grandparents for a couple of years. I remember my grandparents' massive, beautiful house. My granddad built it with his own two hands, and he loved that house.

They sold it a long time ago, because it had become too big for them, but I miss that house a lot.

Nonetheless, a house that was too big for two adults was definitely too big for me as a kid. At nighttime, it was the scariest house on the face of the planet! I couldn't escape the thought that it must be full of ghosts and other hidden dangers.

This was a problem because I was at an age where my parents and grandparents could go out and leave me home alone. But if it got late and I was tired and wanted to go up to my bedroom, I would freak out a bit. Because then, I had to go up the stairs alone, in the dark.

My bedroom was off the top of the staircase. I would climb the stairs, turn right, and walk to the very end of the hallway to my room. The only problem was that the light switch for the staircase was at the bottom of the stairs, and I had to turn it off before heading up.

I don't know about you, but darkness intimidates me, and it was especially ominous in that big house. I remember fretting, "What happens if I get up the stairs and there's an intruder or an evil spirit lying in wait for me?"

Have you ever worried about what's lurking ahead of you, in the darkness of the unknown? That physical darkness terrified me.

So I would stand there with my finger poised on the light switch, which was still turned on. I could see up the stairs, and a little bit into the hallway, yet I remained wary.

Finally, I counted, "One, two—" and before I got to three, I began to run up the stairs, flicking off the lights in the last possible instant as I did so. I ran the whole way up the stairs, turned right, ran all the way to my bedroom, quickly turn the light on, and looked back to make sure there was no one there.

Of course, no one ever was.

It Starts with a Thought

Have you ever done that—the "run in the dark?" When I was standing at the bottom of the stairs, I knew logically there was no one up there. I knew my parents locked the doors when they went out, and it was highly unlikely there was anything scary at the top of my stairs. Yet for some reason, the thought entered my mind, so I had to do the run in the dark.

Fear and anxiety always start with a thought.

King Jehoshaphat, the king of Judah, received word that there were three large armies—each from a populous neighbor—who had joined forces and were marching against him. They were a vast enough host to defeat the Judahite army without even trying, and their purpose was to tear down him and his kingdom:

> *After this the Moabites and Amorites, and with them some of the Midianites, came against Jehoshaphat for battle. Some men came and told Jehoshaphat, "A great multitude is coming against you from Edom, from beyond the sea; and, behold, they are in Hazazon-Tamar" (that is Engedi). Then Jehoshaphat was afraid...* — **2 Chronicles 20:1–3**

Note that the king became afraid at the thought of three large armies coming his way—because fear begins with a thought. In Hebrew, this word 'afraid' is *yirah*, which indicates terror[2] or deep-seated fear. He wasn't just a tiny bit scared. He wasn't even peeing-his-pants scared.

No, he was filled with anxiety and dread, because defeat would mean the end of Judah: he would likely be executed, his people slaughtered or enslaved, and their homes and property seized or destroyed.

Seeds of Fear

Everything in life starts with a seed. Plants, of course, grow from seeds. A corporation grows from investment by its shareholders. Home or car ownership begins with a down payment. And emotions grow from thoughts.

Fear and anxiety are no exceptions. Thoughts are the seeds of anxiety, and they aren't necessarily unreasonable thoughts. For instance, Jehoshaphat had reason to be afraid of the imminent attack on his kingdom by an overwhelming force. Real, external threats sometimes fuel anxiety.

On the other hand, we sometimes allow seeds of anxiety to take root in our hearts and minds based merely on imagined or perceived thoughts, without hard evidence. We become stressed out, afraid, or ashamed based on possibilities that are unlikely or threats that may not exist.

Often these imagined sources of anxiety involve possible thoughts or intentions that other people have toward us, which may be difficult or impossible to ascertain for sure. We might worry, "Why did X unfriend me on Facebook? Oh, no—what if he found out about Y and plans on doing Z?"

The longer we leave a seed in fertile ground and feed it, the more the plant grows. Unfortunately, the same is true with our fear and anxiety. The more we entertain thoughts of a threat or danger, whether real or imagined, and thereby water and nurture it, the more anxious we'll become. If this continues, the source of anxiety will consume our joy and hope, filling our spirit with fear and paralysing us with dread.

Real or Imagined?

The majority of anxiety and fears I've helped people confront are not real and imminent threats. Most of us, myself included, are filled with anxiety over things that exist only in our minds.

Have you ever seen a person look at you in a weird way and thought he or she must dislike you? Perhaps afterward you became filled with anxiety when you encountered that person, because you didn't want to talk to them. Just because of the possible meanings your imagination assigned to an ambiguous glance, you allow anxiety a foothold.

When we have a sore throat, or our body aches, or we're exhausted, many of us are inclined to think we must have a disease. Then we Google our supposed symptoms, which is an especially bad idea. Over the years, I have convinced myself I've had quite a few nasty diseases. Such fears may lack supporting evidence and ultimately prove baseless, but the anxiety we experience is real!

For instance, when I was in Africa many years ago, I played soccer with a little boy after I'd cut my leg.. The field was rough, and he cut his foot whilst playing.

Later, as we coloured on the craft table, he came and sat on my knee and our cuts intertwined. His blood was touching my blood. Initially, I didn't think anything of it.

But later that day, his teacher told me the boy had HIV. Suddenly, it was no longer okay.

I remember thinking, "Oh, my gosh! I've contracted HIV. There is no escape from this. What am I going to do?" I found myself crying my eyes out.

I was in a panic, and it wasn't completely unfounded: another missionary afterward told me he knew of someone else contracting HIV in such a way.

When I was back in Australia, doctors told me: "Oh, don't get tested for three months, because three months is the waiting period and it might not show up until that point."

After three months, I forgot about it. Then, after six months, I got a cold. My body ached a bit. I found this little lump in the roof of my mouth, and I googled my symptoms. Do you know what Google said my symptoms were? HIV.

Anxiety instantly flooded my heart and mind. I was freaking out. I remember muttering in a panic, "I have HIV, I have HIV…"

I went to the doctor and told him something like: "Blood, African kid, HIV! I've got it, you just need to—"

And he said, "We will test you. It's okay. But your symptoms don't sound like HIV."

I told him, "Google told me. Test me now, take as much blood as you need! In fact, take all the blood out! Give me someone else's blood so it's gone!"

He took my blood test, and twenty hours passed. When I was at work the next day, I called the doctor's office and asked if my blood test results had come back.

The lady says yes, but she wasn't allowed to tell me anything because of privacy and confidentiality.

I told her I didn't care about privacy and confidentiality and I was over an hour away, so she should just tell me whether I had HIV or not. She then offered to put me through to the doctor.

After she put me through to the doctor, his first words were that he wanted me to come in. Well, that was impossible right then, because I was at work. But I told him I was guessing by his tone of voice I had HIV, and I asked if could he please just tell me so I wouldn't have to drive for over an hour, crying the whole way.

Though he invoked privacy and confidentiality and repeated that I needed to come in to his office, he also told me I had nothing to worry about.

However, the doctor telling me I had nothing to worry about still had me worried. I tried to read the worst possibilities between the lines of the few words he'd said to me. Thus, as I drove to the doctor's office, I fretted about what drugs they might give me, whether they could manage it or not, and how long I might have to live.

To cut a long story short, I didn't have HIV. But I was filled with anxiety! It seemed like a plausible threat, based on what I read online, but I should have trusted God over Google and waited for the evidence to come in. As soon as evidence became available, my anxiety and fear departed.

If we are to overcome the thoughts that lead to anxiety and fear, we must understand the difference between an insidious, imaginary danger and a genuine, imminent threat. And the difference is this: we can verify a real threat with hard evidence.

For instance, Jehoshaphat had reason to feel anxiety and fear over reports from the field of a hostile army coming to destroy his kingdom and his people. A test result, an eye witness, a hard copy, words actually spoken—those constitute evidence.

Without evidence, all you have are perceived threats and imaginary worries. Countless times, people have asked me, "Is everything okay? Are you and your wife angry or upset at me? Did we do something wrong? Do you hate us?" No, we don't hate you. Those fears are misguided interpretations of mine or my wife's facial expressions.

Being an introverted thinker who doesn't wear her emotions on her sleeve, my wife, Jacqui, often has a neutral expression that others can perceive as very serious. And her serious face sometimes appears to others as being upset or angry. They wonder if they need to apologise to her, when in fact Jacqui isn't upset with anyone! The reality is, she loves everyone—and if she's upset, she won't hesitate to tell you outright!

Don't let your perceptions and your worst fears dictate your reality.

Deal with It!

Whether the threat is imminent like Jehoshaphat's, based on evidence, or full of false information because of a baseless perception or thought, the best time to deal with your thought is now. Don't leave seeds of worry until tomorrow, next week, or next year. Instead, deal with them now—before they sprout into full-fledged anxiety.

The thoughts for which you have evidence may seem relatively straightforward to confront, because we have specific information and can develop a clear action plan for them.

By contrast, the perceptions without evidence can be more intimidating or more difficult to wrap our minds around, especially because we often blow them out of proportion. However, once we roll up our sleeves and begin to tackle these exaggerated or imagined problems head-on, the reality of the situation may become increasingly clear.

Regardless, the best time to deal with seeds of anxiety is today, not tomorrow. It's better to find freedom in the beginning than to be trapped for years, only afterward realising you had the keys in your hand the whole time. Do we truly want to live with that kind of regret?

We may have painful episodes in our personal history, and others may have hurt us at one time or another, but the best time to confront the pain and accompanying anxiety is now. We don't have to continue suffering and worrying about what's happened to us or what might happen to us.

Moreover, as mentioned previously, the Word of God tells us not to "be anxious about anything" (Philippians 4:6). Then, in verse 8, we find instructions for the alternative to anxiety:

Finally, brothers whatever is true, whatever is honorable, whatever is just, whatever is pure, whatever is lovely, whatever is commendable, if there is anything of excellence, if there is anything worthy of praise, think about these things.

Some people decontextualise verse 8 and present it as a standalone verse about thinking holy and pure thoughts. Yes, we should think holy and pure thoughts, but that's not the extent of this scripture's meaning. This verse is addressing anxiety, as we know from the command against anxiety that prefaced it in verse 6.

Therefore, the entirety of God's command to us regarding anxiety boils down to this: Instead of worrying, think about pure and holy things. But, how do we stop worrying?

The seed of anxiety is always a fearful thought. To deal with and take control of anxiety, we must trap those fearful thoughts and set against them the kinds of thoughts Paul listed in Philippians 4.

Taking Thoughts Captive

It's time to trap the thoughts that have been trapping us. Anxious and fearful thoughts hold us captive, but we are to turn the tables. As Paul explains in 2 Corinthians 10:5, "We destroy arguments and every lofty opinion raised against the knowledge of God, and take every thought captive to obey Christ."

Thoughts are to be our captives, not the other way around! The word 'captive' means a prisoner or a slave—in essence, someone who is trapped.

Moreover, this verse says we ought to "destroy arguments" and opinions that contradict God's Word. Because God's Word instructs us not to be anxious, then, we must consciously eliminate anxious thoughts. We must trap them and enslave them to the truth.

This is what Jehoshaphat did, according to 2 Chronicles. Instead of allowing his fearful thoughts of the invading armies to take root and grow in his mind, worrying about the destruction of his reign and his people, he focussed on God and turned the situation over to Him:

And Jehoshaphat stood in the assembly of Judah and Jerusalem, in the house of the LORD, before the new court, (He didn't just do this on his own. He stood up in front of everyone who knew that the armies were coming their way. He stood up in front of everyone who knew there was a threat on its way. He stood up in front of everyone who knew they were doomed, who knew that come nightfall they were probably going to be dead) *and said, "O LORD, God of our fathers, are you not God in heaven? You rule over all the kingdoms of the nations. In your hand are power and might, so that none is able to withstand you. Did you not, our God, drive out the inhabitants of this land before your people Israel, and give it forever to the descendants of Abraham your friend? And they have lived in it and built for you in it a sanctuary for your name, saying, 'If disaster comes upon us, the sword, judgment, or pestilence, or famine, we will stand before this house and before you—for your name is in this house—and cry out to you in our affliction, and you will hear and save.' And now behold, the men of Ammon and Moab and Mount Seir, whom you would not let Israel invade when they came from the land of Egypt, and whom they avoided and did not destroy— behold, they reward us by coming to drive us out of your possession, which you have given us to inherit. O our God, will you not execute judgment on them? For we are powerless against this great horde that is coming against us. We do not know what to do, but our eyes are on you."* — **2 Chronicles 20:5–12**

Some of us have anxiety or fear that obstructs everything God wants for us. Though we claim to have faith in God, we may balk at trusting Him with the threats, (real or imagined), that confront us. To dispel the deep-rooted fears and anxiety trying to grip our hearts and minds, however, we can look to the testimonies of God's power and faithfulness found in the Word and in the lives of our fellow Christ-followers.

The Power Of Testimony

King Jehoshaphat reached back to the testimony of his people's relationship with God and pulled out the truth of God's promises. Though the king spoke his thoughts of an imminent, life-and-death threat, he also countered the seed of anxiety by speaking the truth about his God.

Jehoshaphat remembered the God of Abraham who had brought them into the land, who helped them defeat enemy armies in the past, and he knew God could do it again. The king of Judah told God he knew He had helped His people possess the land then, and he knew He would help them keep the land now.

Sometimes, like Jehoshaphat, we need to ride on the testimonies of God conveyed to us by others, past or present. When the book of Revelation looks back at how the church and the people of God overcame the enemy, it says, "And they overcame him by the blood of the Lamb and by the word of their testimony..." (Revelation 12:11). Clearly, the "word of your testimony" is powerful to vanquish the forces of wickedness and deception!

With this in mind, when God helps us through difficult circumstances, we ought to praise Him for it. But we shouldn't limit ourselves to praising Him for it quietly, as we sit alone and pray, "Thank you, Jesus." Instead, let's thank Jesus publicly!

Be willing and ready to share with others, "I was facing this awful trial, but God did something far greater than I could ever think, perceive, or dream, and He brought me out of it!" Then don't be surprised if someone who is enduring a similar situation looks at you and tells you they needed to hear that encouragement. They needed their faith to be strengthened.

Thus, some of us need to share our testimony, but we also need to ride on other people's testimonies. We must hold onto the stories of God's greatness and how He overcame all sorts of threats to those who trusted in Him. Then we can say with confidence:

"God, I know You healed this person who had this sickness, and I know You can heal me in my situation."

"God, I know You provided for the person in this situation, so I know You will help me find a job."

"God, I know You have restored this family, this marriage, or this friendship, so even though the divorce papers are already on my office table, I know You can heal this relationship."

When we trap our seeds of fear and anxiety and submit them to testimony of God, our perceptions of our circumstances, of other people, and of God Himself are transformed. As we speak God's Word over our situation and remind ourselves of His promises, anxiety fades, fear dissipates, and the way forward becomes clear.

Some friends of mine post Scripture on the doors and mirrors of their bathroom. The Lord's Prayer is on the door, and every time I use the bathroom, I pray the Lord's Prayer. When I wash my hands, I read the verses all over the mirror.

We should be putting up verses around our bathrooms and bedrooms. We should be adding scriptures onto our smartphone calendars, reminders, and to-do lists. We should even be tucking Bible verses into the sun visors in our cars so they fall in our lap when we lower the visor! One way or another, we must be taking specific action and adopting specific habits on a daily basis, to remind ourselves of God's thoughts and promises.

Sharing Our Struggles

When my wife and I were planting our church, there was a period when we both experienced great anxiety. In fact, both of us lost a lot of weight due to the stress—which may sound like it was a good thing, at least in my case, but anxiety is not a healthy way to shed weight!

Why were we so anxious? People were gossiping about us and spreading rumours. In my heart, I knew that relationships with some of our friends had been destroyed. Some of the people whom we had held closest to us now weren't there for us, which brought me great distress.

I wasn't sleeping well, and the anxiety even caused acne to break out all over my face. At night I spent time mired in worry about what to do.

What if these stories and lies about us filtered out to other people and destroyed our credibility? What if, as a consequence, the community dismissed our new church as a joke? What if people looked at our ministry and thought we were frauds who couldn't possibly be used by God? What if no one would so much as talk to us anymore?

At one point, we caught up with some pastor friends of ours. We got together over lunch to get advice on church planting.

Right as we stepped into the café with them, however, I received a troubling text message from someone. As we sat down to eat, I found myself unable to listen to what our friends said because I was so distracted by the message I had received on my phone.

Finally, I apologised and told our friends I didn't even know what they were talking about because this text had just come through.

In response, one of our friends shared that a very similar situation had occurred when he was planting his church. Yet in the end, despite all that transpired, he successfully planted a growing church that was reaching the lost and broken. Hearing his testimony helped me realise there was hope in my situation, too.

I wondered why the people who wrote books and developed courses about church planting never talked about these sorts of trials. Why didn't they say they had people who stabbed them in the back, or had their best friends turn and walk away?

As I spoke with more church planters and people who led thriving churches, each one said the same situation had happened to them. When they related their stories, I was able to trap my fears, replace them with thoughts of God's surpassing greatness, and see my anxiety fade away.

As Paul wrote to the Ephesians, "For our struggle is not against flesh and blood, but against the rulers, against the authorities, against the powers of this dark world" (Ephesians 6:12). My fellow church-planters' testimonies reminded me that we are not supposed to preoccupy ourselves bickering and contending amongst each other. My old best friends were not my enemies, despite our recent differences.

The true enemy, our spiritual enemy, had infected the relationship somehow, and as a result our former friends were talking badly about us. But I still loved them. Even now, I still hold them dear, and I hope one day God will restore the broken relationships.

Regardless, my anxiety is gone. I know no matter what comes my way or what people say about me, God will build His church and make a way forward for His people.

Breaking the Yoke

Jesus said, "Truly, I say to you, whatever you bind on earth shall be bound in heaven, and whatever you loose on earth shall be loosed in heaven" (Matthew 18:18).

Some of us have loosed ungodly thoughts, and they take over our mind, our hearts, and our spirit. Then anxiety fills us, becomes a burden, and weighs us down.

The book of Isaiah offered many prophecies about Jesus long before He came to earth. And Isaiah 10:27 says this: "He will break the yoke of slavery and lift it from their shoulders" (NLT). The yoke was an apparatus used to link two oxen or other animals pulling a cart or plow so one wouldn't be able to go faster than the other—they would walk at the same speed.

Some of us have yoked or connected ourselves to our anxious and fearful thoughts, and we have thereby allowed them to define our thinking and our lives. We can't go out into public places, because we are scared. We don't want to join groups of other Christ-followers, because we are intimidated by other people and what they might think of us or how they might react to us.

Stop yoking yourself to such imagined threats, which are seeds of anxiety, and instead let Jesus set you free! Allow Him to break the yoke of your enslavement to fear. Let Him fill you with His thoughts about you and His plans for you.

We must declare ourselves children of God, created in His image, and place our hope in Him. We must oppose and trap the fearful thoughts and lies of the enemy with the Word of God and testimony of His goodness. It's a process that begins with trapping the thought—and ends in victory.

Chapter 2 Notes

WORKBOOK

Chapter 2 Questions

Question: When have you experienced a deep-rooted anxiety as a result of a thought? How did the thought first arise?

_____

_____

_____

_____

_____

_____

_____

_____

_____

_____

_____

Question: How have you allowed an anxious thought or fear to grow? In what ways did it rob you of joy and hope in your daily life?

_____

_____

_____

_____

_____

_____

_____

_____

_____

_____

Question: What is the difference between a false, intrusive thought and a real, imminent threat? With which type do you most often struggle? Why?

_____

_____

_____

_____

_____

_____

_____

_____

_____

Question: How did Jehoshaphat take his thoughts captive? What are ways you could follow his example?

_____

_____

_____

_____

_____

_____

_____

_____

_____

_____

_____

Question: Why does hearing testimony of how God has worked give us hope? How can you take specific steps to remind yourself of testimonies from the Bible? What testimony do you need to share, and with whom?

_____

_____

_____

_____

_____

_____

_____

_____

_____

_____

_____

Action: Begin taking your fearful thoughts captive instead of letting them grow! Re-read the story of Jehoshaphat, paying close attention to when he started to fear, and to how he overcame that fear by turning to God. Share a testimony about God's work through a trying time in your life with someone else this week.

Chapter 2 Notes

_____

_____

_____

_____

_____

_____

_____

_____

_____

_____

_____

_____

_____

_____

_____

_____

_____

_____

_____

_____

_____

_____

_____

_____

_____

CHAPTER THREE

Turn Your Head

I will confess, I loved Winnie the Pooh when I was young. My favourite character was Piglet, whose timidity and distinctive stutter I found amusing.

In particular, I recall the old Disney cartoon "Winnie the Pooh and the Blustery Day," which was based on episodes from the original Pooh books. Winnie the Pooh and Piglet were walking through the Hundred Acre Wood, but it became very windy. Whenever the wind picked up, Piglet would fly into the air, so Pooh had to hold Piglet.

This experience was especially stressful for Piglet, of course, who worried that the windstorm would knock a tree down and crush the pair. Filled with anxiety, Piglet stuttered:

> "Oh dear, supposing a tree fell down, Pooh, when we were underneath it?"

"Supposing it didn't," said Pooh. After careful thought, Piglet was comforted by this.[3]

Pooh might not have been the most brilliant bear ever, but he had a calmer temperament and a more balanced perspective than Piglet did—at least, when his rumbly tummy wasn't involved. By contrast, Piglet's anxiety distorted his perspective on the situation.

Opposing Viewpoints

The way we see the world and other people—that is, our perspective or viewpoint—dictates our emotions, thoughts and behaviour. From Piglet's perspective, the wind was the most significant element, so he became frightened. By contrast, Pooh was more aware of his hunger and the thought of his pot of honey sitting in his house, so he was ready to brave the wind to reach it.

Likewise, you and I could stand right next to each other, looking at the same thing, but perceiving them differently. And our actions and our lives would be influenced by our respective perceptions, accordingly.

After all, this is one reason why police officers try to interview multiple witnesses at the scene of an accident. Each driver or bystander perceives the event from his or her distinctive vantage point, so the police gather the various stories from the different observers and piece them together to get a more complete picture.

I'm not arguing that we each live in our own reality or our own dimension, no matter what science fiction or superhero movies might lead us to believe. There is an objective reality. But only God is omniscient, so only He has a complete, holistic perception and understanding of that reality.

Filtered Lenses

In other words, we don't see things as they are—we see things as we are. We see things based on the lens through which we filter every observation. Our unique minds, personalities, priorities, and sets of experiences lead us to view and respond to our environments, interactions, and information in different ways.

No matter how analytical, educated, rational, scientific, or objective we might be, we've each got our own personal lens. It comprises our genetics and our childhood, our culture and religion, our faith and values, our current circumstances, and more.

The interaction of those elements determines how we filter our world and our experiences to produce particular thoughts. And it determines how we respond.

Our personal baggage is part of this. If you were bullied in school, or if a loved one has walked out on you, you will tend to filter your life through the lens of someone who has experienced those kinds of pain or rejection.

Moreover, all of us today doubtless view many things differently from the way King Jehoshaphat and the Judahites viewed their ancient biblical world. But we have one thing in common: our lens must include God's Word.

Watching the Problems

Too often, our lens is clouded with anxiety. Yet the Bible instructs us in Philippians 4:6 not to be anxious— not about anything! As we discussed in the introduction to this book, this prohibition against worry is a command, not a suggestion.

Moreover, what good does it do to worry? As Jesus said, "And which of you by being anxious can add a single hour to his span of life?" (Matthew 6:27).

In fact, researchers have discovered connections between various levels of stress and increased risk of death.[4] After all, God designed us, so He knows better than anyone what's bad for our health!

Jehoshaphat trapped his anxious and fearful thoughts as he recounted what God had done and what He could do. Sure, the king could have dwelt on how huge the army was. He could have sat inside his palace and watched out the window as the armies approached, looming ever larger. He could have acted like Denethor, the steward of Gondor in Tolkien's *The Return of the King*, who saw the host of Mordor approach his city and despaired.

Sometimes, like Denethor, we spend too much time looking at the problem, watching it grow and giving all of our attention to this source of our anxiety and fear. When we are not searching for a solution, but instead obsess about the problem itself, we feed it—and it grows. Over time, we create a monster in our life.

Thankfully for Judah, Jehoshaphat didn't sit there and watch the problem coming over the horizon. Second Chronicles 20:3 explains, "Then Jehoshaphat was afraid and set his face to seek the Lord." The king turned his face from looking at the problem. He lifted his eyes off of the current circumstances—off of the apparently hopeless military predicament—and redirected his attention toward God. And Jehoshaphat declared to Him:

"We do not know what to do, but our eyes are on you. "

Meanwhile all Judah stood before the LORD, with their little ones, their wives, and their children. And the spirit of the LORD came upon Jahaziel the son of Zechariah, son of Benaiah, son of Jeiel, son of Mattaniah, a Levite of the sons of Asaph, in the midst of the assembly. And he said (the spirit of the LORD said through this man), *"Listen, all Judah and inhabitants of Jerusalem and King Jehoshaphat: Thus says the LORD to you, 'Do not be afraid and do not be dismayed at this great horde, for the battle is not yours but God's. Tomorrow go down against them. Behold, they will come up by the ascent of Ziz. You will find them at the end of the valley, east of the wilderness of Jeruel. You will not need to fight in this battle. Stand firm, hold your position, and see the salvation of the LORD on your behalf, O Judah and Jerusalem.' Do not be afraid and do not be dismayed. Tomorrow go out against them, and the LORD will be with you."* — *2 Chronicles 20:12–17*

When anxiety and fear fill our mind, and all we can see is the problem, we need to turn our head and fix our eyes on the solution. We must look to the One who holds our life in His hands, the King of kings and Lord of lords.

That is, we must turn our heads toward Jesus. For He is the One who:

- calms storms (Mark 4:35–41)

- feeds the multitudes (Matthew 14:13–21)
- spoke the universe into existence (Hebrews 11:3)
- cares enough for us to know the very hairs on our head (Luke 12:7)
- voluntarily endured the shame and pain of death on a cross to redeem us from our sins

Jesus can bring hope to our most dire-seeming situations. We don't need to look at our problems, which will only keep weighing us down. Instead, we need to look at the only One who can truly get us out of our predicaments.

As Jehoshaphat said in 2 Chronicles 20:12, "We do not know what to do, but our eyes are on you." Too often, we attempt our own, ultimately inadequate solutions as a first resort, and only turn to God when all else fails. But if we maintain an eternal perspective, we will learn to turn our heads first and trust in Him from the start.

It's All About Perspective

On that blustery day, Piglet focussed on his current problem (the wind) while Pooh took his eyes off the problem and focussed on his solution (home and a pot of honey). The nation of Judah could have fretted about the invading armies, but instead they looked to their solution, God.

Many of us are like Piglet and need an adjustment of our perspective in viewing our experiences. We need to switch to a lens that allows us to see in accordance with God's perspective.

Either we can look at the source of our anxiety, whether it be a real threat or a perceived threat, or we can look at God, who has all power in the situation. As the psalmist says in Psalm 121:2, "My help comes from the LORD, the Maker of heaven and earth" (NIV).

Indeed, "the Maker of heaven and earth" trumps all alternatives in our moments of greatest need. Because if He can make heaven and the earth, He can make a way forward amidst our circumstances.

What Happens When You Look to God?

Thus, when Jehoshaphat "set his face to seek the LORD ... [and] Judah assembled to seek help from the LORD" (2 Chronicles 20:3–4), they were admitting they didn't know what to do. However, they were also acknowledging that God was capable of addressing their situation. In other words, "We don't know what to do, God, so we'll look to you!"

As a result, the Spirit of God spoke into their situation. When we look to God, He speaks into our life and shares what is on His heart for us.

And His message to the Judahites was similar to what He says to us when anxiety fills our lives: "Do not be afraid and do not be dismayed at this great horde, for the battle is not yours but God's" (2 Chronicles 20:15). God told them to stop thinking they had to fight the enemy on their own. They were His children, as we are, and so it was never their fight to begin with—it was His.

In those days, the king would lead the army into battle. So God was saying, in effect, "Hang on a second!

Remember, I am King. I am the one who will lead you into battle, because I protect My children—My nation and My people. Stop worrying.

"For no matter what happens, I am the Lord, and I will ensure everything works out for the best. If you love Me and trust Me, and if you faithfully live out the purposes I have planned for you, then there's no cause for worry" (see Romans 8:28).

Then God's instruction continued:

Tomorrow go down against them. Behold, they will come up by the ascent of Ziz. You will find them at the end of the Valley, east of the wilderness of Jeruel. — 2 Chronicles 20:16

Wait a moment! Didn't God just say the problem was His—that "the battle is not yours but God's"? And now He was saying, "Tomorrow go down against them..." How can God say He has the battle covered, then send us into battle? Why must we be involved? Shouldn't God take over and run with it?

There's a crucial distinction between dealing with a situation and facing it. God wants us to face the threats coming against us. He will deal with them, yes, but He doesn't wave a wand and make them vanish. Hostile armies don't suddenly transform into lollipops, rainbows, and fluffy cottontails. That's not how He operates.

There is a popular misconception that Christians are always happy. The truth is, we are filled with joy regardless of circumstances, but this is not because we don't have problems, deny their reality, or wish them out of existence. Rather, we are joyous because in His joy is our strength (Nehemiah 8:10). Our light hearts come from confidence in His ability and willingness to fight for us.

Nonetheless, as for Jehoshaphat and his warriors, we must confront the source of our fear and anxiety head on, keeping our eyes on God as we do so. We must walk toward our problems, not palm them off to God and race for the door. No, even better—we get a front-row seat to God's victory on our behalf.

Just Stand Firm

A word of warning: walking toward the issue won't scare the situation off. It won't frighten the enemy armies away. In fact, they'll keep marching in your direction.

Threats sometimes rear their heads in defiance when we take a stand. But as God assured the Judahites, "Stand firm, hold your position, and see the salvation of the LORD on your behalf, O Judah and Jerusalem. Do not be afraid and do not be dismayed. Tomorrow go out against them" (2 Chronicles 20:15–16).

Though God offered encouragement and a promise, He also required courage and faith of His people. Surely the Judahites experienced some wobbly legs and felt the urge to run from the mighty host arrayed against them. And Jehoshaphat himself perhaps toyed with the possibility of flight or surrender.

Similarly, in our darkest moments, we will want to try to fix the problem ourselves. If there's an approaching army of bloodthirsty invaders (or unscrupulous colleagues) bent on our destruction, we'll be tempted to cut a deal or join their alliance, no matter how wicked. If we're feeling lonely, we might be tempted to involve ourselves in intimate relations with someone outside of God's prescriptions for marriage.

However, God's Word makes His intentions and instructions clear. He didn't tell Jehoshaphat to make an alliance with the enemy. Rather, He simply told the Judahites to stand firm before the enemy.

Likewise, we must face our sources of fear and anxiety without trying to fight or fix them by our own wisdom or design. Instead, God wants us to trust in Him. He wants us to loosen the reins of control, hand over our situation and stand firm.

This principle reminds me of a friend of mine from America. When he visited Australia and I drove him places, he instinctively sat in the passenger seat (which is the driver's seat in an American car) and tried to drive the car, even though I had the wheel.

When I put my car in reverse to back up the hill to my garage, he cried out, "Whoa, whoa, whoa, whoa!" I told him to calm down, because I've performed this particular manoeuvre dozens of times.

Moreover, my car has a rear-view camera, which my friend might not have known the first time he experienced this rapid reverse move. In any case, he thought I was about to hit the garage door, so he grabbed hold of me and yelled at me to stop.

I assured him I saw the garage door just fine and advised he stop trying to control the situation. Regardless of where steering wheels are located in the United States, I had the wheel.

That's more or less what God says to us sometimes: "Stop being a backseat driver. Either let Me take control, or don't have Me at all."

God wants us to stake out a position and stand firm. We must learn to stand in the midst of our pain, heartache, sickness, and betrayal. We must stand in the midst of gossip, joblessness, global terror, and financial crisis. Let's stand in the midst of it all and resist the urge to do anything else. If we stand our ground and keep our eyes fixed on God no matter the outcome, we will always have the victory.

Outcome Versus Victory

There is a difference between outcome and victory. Sometimes we want things to go a certain way—but of course, they don't. Not every prayer we send up to God in heaven gets answered the way we want it to. But when we stand firm, whatever the immediate outcome is, ultimately it's a victory if we trust in Him. It might not look or feel like a victory at the time, but it is.

We naturally place a great deal of focus on these eighty or ninety years we might live. As a consequence, we tend to regard the problems we face as enormous. However, if we consider life from an eternal mindset, our days on earth are barely a blip on the radar—and our problems wouldn't even show up.

From His eternal perspective, God must wonder
sometimes why we get so caught up in those problems of
ours: "Aaron, why are you in such a panic because
Google says you might have a disease?

"I can see the bigger picture. These incidents and episodes in your life serve a larger purpose. It might not
look like a victory from where you're standing, but when
you come home to be with Me, you'll see."

Fixing Our Eyes on Jesus

*Therefore, since we are surrounded by so great a cloud of
witnesses, let us also lay aside every weight, and sin which
clings so closely, and let us run with endurance the race
that is set before us, looking to Jesus, the founder and perfecter of our faith, who for the joy that was set before him
endured the cross, despising the shame, and is seated at the
right hand of the throne of God. — Hebrews 12:1–2*

This scripture remains one of my favorite verses in
the whole Bible: "Therefore, since we are surrounded by
such a great cloud of witnesses, let us also lay aside every weight..."

When anxieties are dragging us down, weighing
heavy on our shoulders, we need to lay them aside and
"shake it off," as Taylor Swift sings.[5] The writer of Hebrews directs us in no uncertain terms to lay down our
sin, which includes any distractions from God's calling,
purpose, and destiny for our lives.

Thus, we must shake off the dead weight and persist
in God's plan for us—running "with endurance the race
that is set before us..." That is, do as God's Word and

His Spirit direct you, whether that's advancing against your problems or holding your ground tenaciously in spite of them.

And all the while, we must be "looking to Jesus." Would we stare at our feet while running a footrace? No, we would focus on the finish line. It's critical to maintain focus on the One who is guiding and shaping the race.

Therefore, keep your eyes on Jesus, who is the "founder," or "author" (NKJV), of your life. He built your life from the ground up. He wrote you into existence. Yes, you have a part to play, but He has written the script and knows what will happen.

Even though each of us is only one of billions of people on the face of the planet, He cares about each of us and knows our individual story personally. And because He is also the "perfecter," when things go wrong He applies His grace to your situation and realigns it with God's plan.

When we veer off of our track, He reroutes us. When we become consumed by worry and anxiety, He can liberate us and resolve the threat at hand. Your problems are nothing to Jesus' perfect power and perspective.

Similarly, the verse says, Jesus endured the cross "for the joy that was set before him." When He approached the cross, as He went to die for you and me, He had His eyes fixed on something. He didn't fix them on the pain as they drove the nails through His hands and feet. He didn't fix them on the people who spat on Him and insulted Him.

He didn't fix them on any aspect of the problem—instead, He fixed His eyes firmly on the end goal, which was the joy of redemption and life for you and me.

Death may look like the end, but often it's the start of the victory. It gives birth to a new phase of God's perfect plan. Though Jesus died on the cross, He is now seated at the right hand of God. The eternal perspective in Hebrews 12 makes clear that if we turn our heads and keep our eyes focussed on Him, rather than on our present anxiety, we'll endure to experience the final triumph.

All Is Well

What besides Jesus has captured your gaze? From what do you need to remove your eyes so you can focus on Him?

The longer our mind lingers on the difficulty of our circumstances, allowing anxiety and dread to fill us, the worse our problem will grow. Hence, we must promptly trap the initial thought and then direct our attention to the Maker of heaven and earth. Let us pray, "No matter the situation and no matter the obstacles at hand, 'through it all, my eyes are on You.' I am not fixing them on the problem anymore, because You are greater."[6]

The song from which I just quoted—"It Is Well"—holds a special place in my life.

When Jacqui and I found out she was pregnant with our second child, we were excited. Then, right about the time we were preparing to announce it to our friends and family, Jacqui woke me up in the middle of the night and said she thought something was wrong. We didn't know what to do, and the doctor's clinic wasn't open so we had to wait until the morning.

That whole night, "It Is Well" was playing on repeat in the background. My heart was filled with anxiety for this child we wanted, whom we loved already. The possibility of it not existing anymore was overwhelming. We were crying in bed, and I was praying that the baby would live. I remember thinking, "God, if this is something serious, step in and help us."

We Googled, though we should have known better, and found that Jacqui's symptoms could be a sign of miscarriage. It could also be a sign of less serious conditions with nothing to worry about. So we convinced ourselves not to worry.

Then I determined to put that particular lyric—"through it all, my eyes are on You"—into practice. I prayed, "God, whether the baby lives or whether it dies, my eyes will stay on You. I believe You can step in, but if not, it's well. It is well with my soul.

"My eyes are staying on You because I know You've got a plan. I know You've got a purpose, Father, and You see this from a different perspective than I do. You are the only one with a perfect lens. All of us have broken lenses. We see everything filtered through our own limited experiences.

"But I don't want to see this situation through my lens anymore—I want to see it through Yours. So God, 'through it all, my eyes are on You.'"

When we went in the next day to get the ultrasound, I prayed as they searched for the baby's heartbeat we had heard on previous visits. I asked God for us to hear its heartbeat again, because I knew He could make it happen.

But it didn't. We had lost the baby. I wish I could say this was a miracle story—that God did what I wanted Him to do and the outcome was exactly as I had planned.

But it didn't turn out the way I thought it was meant to be.

Yet, no matter the outcome, Jacqui and I know we are prepared for victory, because there is victory when we turn our head from the problem and keep our eyes fixed on Jesus.

WORKBOOK

Chapter 3 Questions

Question: What baggage do you carry with you that negatively impacts your point of view?

_____

_____

_____

_____

_____

_____

_____

_____

_____

_____

Question: How can you start to redirect your mind toward God and His Word when you start to become fearful or anxious?

_____

_____

_____

_____

_____

_____

_____

_____

_____

_____

_____

Question: Why does God want us to face trials and difficulties directly instead of taking them away from us?

_____

_____

_____

_____

_____

_____

_____

_____

_____

_____

_____

Question: What does standing firm in the Lord look like in the face of fear, problems, or challenges?

_____

_____

_____

_____

_____

_____

_____

_____

_____

_____

_____

_____

Question: What situation, fear, or anxiety is causing you to take your eyes off Jesus? How does reflecting on what Jesus endured on the cross spur you to keep your eyes on God?

_____

_____

_____

_____

_____

_____

_____

_____

_____

_____

_____

Action: Turn your head—toward God! Spend time reflecting on what it would look like to stand firm in the Lord through a current trial you're experiencing. Pray to God and ask Him to help you to trust Him in difficulties and when things aren't going the way you had hoped. Meditate on Hebrews 12:1–2, then draft your own paraphrase of the passage.

Chapter 3 Notes

_____

_____

_____

_____

_____

_____

_____

_____

_____

_____

_____

_____

_____

_____

_____

_____

_____

_____

_____

_____

_____

_____

CHAPTER FOUR

Train Your Tongue

We live in age of social media, where you can post anything and everything on the internet, amass instant followers, or have your post go "viral."

For those of you who are into looking up hashtags (for the uninitiated, that means topic keywords signified by a #) on Instagram, '#anxiety' has been used in over 4 million posts. And many additional posts can be found under '#anxietydisorder.'

As I looked at some of the posts related to anxiety recently, I realised how overwhelming this problem has become in our world today. Our society is plagued daily with anxiety and fear.

And that's not just people outside of the church walls, either. People in the church are experiencing deep anxiety and fear, too.

The people of God, however, are supposed to respond differently to anxiety and fear.

Corrie ten Boom understood this. She was a young Dutch Christian whose family helped hide Jews fleeing Nazi persecution during the Holocaust. Eventually, Corrie and her family were arrested as part of the Dutch Resistance, and she and her sister Betsy ended up in a concentration camp together, where Betsy died.

Corrie afterward recalled that praise proved necessary to endure her sister's death and the harrowing experience of the camp. She declared:

> Praise will sweeten and hallow all that it touches.
>
> Praise will kindle a new faith.
>
> Praise will fan the sparks of a smoldering love into a flame of love for God.
>
> Praise will start the joy bell ringing in your soul.
>
> Praise will pierce through the darkness.
>
> Praise will dynamite away long-standing obstruction.
>
> Praise will strike terror in the heart of Satan.[7]

Corrie ten Boom understood that we are to train our tongues with praise.

A Language of Praise

Training your tongue isn't just a matter of refraining from profanity or crude speech. Far more than that, it's about getting your tongue in the habit of speaking a new language—a language of praise.

Our churches these days have a lot of prayer going on, which is of course important, but it must be coupled with praise and thanksgiving. The Bible says that instead of being anxious, "by prayer and supplication with thanksgiving let your request be made known to God" (Philippians 4:6).

If the entire church realised the power of praising God instead of only coming to Him and asking for things all the time, it would be a game changer. There is power in praising Him, and we can use that language rather than limiting ourselves to approaching Him on our hands and knees in desperation.

Sometimes when we speak things in a praiseworthy manner, it accomplishes greater things than when we merely ask for something.

We see this in the case of King Jehoshaphat, who responded obediently to the will of God by leading his people out to face the enemy. Before he did so, according to 2 Chronicles 20:18, "King Jehoshaphat bowed his head with his face to the ground, and all Judah and the inhabitants of Jerusalem fell before the LORD, worshiping the LORD." Everyone in Judah fell down and worshiped God!

Sometimes we do all God has asked us to do, down to the letter, and make sure we say the right things and avoid any behavior that would upset Him or further distance ourselves from Him. Yet our anxiety continues to flare up in the face of our problems—and that's where praise comes into play.

Reaching God's Presence in Praise and Worship

We need to train our tongue in this new language of praise and worship. We need to train our tongue to do something that doesn't seem natural or right to our physical senses. Our human perspective protests, "No, you are facing an imminent threat and you've got to fix it *now*!"

But we must remember to keep our minds focussed on God. We must do everything God tells us to do, and then go out to face our trials with praise on our lips. King Jehoshaphat seems to have understood the power of praise, because he led with worship.

Moreover, we read in Psalm 22:3: "Yet you are holy, enthroned on the praises of Israel." As another translation phrases it, God makes His "home on the praises of Israel" (VOICE). God dwells, lives, and resides in the praises of His people! There is power when we worship and praise because God's presence lives and overflows in our worship.

When Jesus died on the cross, He exclaimed these words: "It is finished." (John 19:30). In the temple, a heavy curtain tore in two, which symbolises the way God's presence was no longer confined to the church or temple anymore. It was accessible to you and me.

Now every moment of every day, we are able to access God's presence in our lives. We don't have to be a priest or perform any rituals to experience God, because Jesus died on the cross to neutralise our sin—every errant thought and "little white lie" that separated us from His presence.

As Jesus died on the cross, He took away our sin, shame, and blemishes. And when He rose again, the sin didn't rise with Him.

If we choose to follow Jesus, we must repent and turn away from our sins, ask Jesus to make us clean and whole, and chase after His plan for our lives. Then we can experience God's presence, which praise and worship invite into our lives even in our most dire and anxious moments.

Remember to Believe

The story of King Jehoshaphat continues:

And the Levites, of the Kohathites and the Korahites, stood up to praise the LORD, the God of Israel, with a very loud voice.

And they rose early in the morning and went out into the wilderness of Tekoa. And when they went out, Jehoshaphat stood and said, "Hear me, Judah and inhabitants of Jerusalem! Believe in the LORD your God, and you will be established; believe his prophets, and you will succeed.
— 2 Chronicles 20:19–20

Sometimes when everything is coming against us, we need to be encouraged and reminded to believe in God. Maybe there is one situation in which we simply find it hard to have faith because we question where God has been all this time. Why hasn't He helped us already?

Sometimes we need to be reminded that God is faithful and we can believe in Him. If we establish and build our life around our trust in God, that's a strong good foundation of faith from which He will operate on our behalf.

Belief in God will establish us and help us build our life well. And when we believe in the holy words and testimony of godly people who surround us and speak encouragement into our life, that will also help us succeed. Others' encouragement will help us face and conquer those things coming against us.

Praise Needs to Come First

Thus, we read in 2 Chronicles 20:21:

> *And when he had taken counsel with the people, he appointed those who were to sing to the LORD and praise him in holy attire, as they went before the army, and say, "Give thanks to the LORD, for his steadfast love endures forever."*

When we face a situation or problem causing anxiety in our life, praise needs to be our first resort. Before we plan to get a lawyer, a new job, take all our money out of a bank account, sign legal documents, exchange words with someone, or move to a new house, we need to praise God. We must learn to be fluent in the language of praise, declaring reflexively but sincerely that God is great.

He is greater than our circumstances and needs, and we can give thanks to Him, "for His steadfast love endures forever" (Psalm 136:1). In other words, we give thanks to the God whose love has always been there for us.

God's love has always dealt with situations in a good way, for the best for people—working "for the good for those who love Him and are called according to his purpose for them" (Romans 8:28 NLT).

His love is reliable and can be trusted because He is the same God "yesterday, today, and forever" (Hebrews 13:8). Thus, we don't have to worry about our situation. Instead, we can focus on giving thanks, knowing He's got it in His hands whether it all works out the way we want or not. We only need to concern ourselves with praising Him for the here and now, and for the victory that is to come.

Second Chronicles 20:22–23 adds:

> *And when they began to sing and praise, the LORD set an ambush against the men of Ammon, Moab, and Mount Seir, who had come against Judah, so that they were routed. For the men of Ammon and Moab rose against the inhabitants of Mount Seir, devoting them to destruction, and when they had made an end of the inhabitants of Seir, they all helped to destroy one another.*

When the people from Judah praised and gave thanks to the Lord, God sent an ambush to destroy the three armies coming against them. We don't know what the ambush looked like or who perpetrated it, but suddenly these three armies were thrown into confusion and they turned on one another. The armies annihilated each other instead of annihilating God's people.

Note that it wasn't until the Judahites sang, that God sent the ambush. God had lots of time before then to send the ambush. It may have been days since Jehoshaphat found out the armies were coming against him. Then they set out, they did what God told them to do, and walked toward the valley where they would battle.

Though God had a lot of time to work with, for some reason He waited until they began to sing and praise.

Some of us need to praise God, and then something will happen. So often when problems come our way, we complain, whine, or question why it is happening. We blame God or become angry with Him and fail to see Him—all while claiming to do everything He wants us to do.

Maybe we simply need to train our tongue in the language that isn't complaining, going to a pity party, or wallowing in grief, but instead is giving praise regardless of less than ideal circumstances. Even though it doesn't make sense, we are directed to offer thanks to the God whose "love endures forever" (Psalm 136:1) and who is holding us "in His hands" (Job 12:10).

The Battle Is His

When God tells us the battle is His and the victory is sure if we trust in Him, we should face the enemy with a song of thanks.

Our anxieties and fears often execute themselves in God's presence as we praise Him. God's plan for your life and my life rests on a spirit of strength, not fear. He says He didn't give us "a spirit of fear but one of power, strength, love, and sound judgment" (2 Timothy 1:7 CSB).

God doesn't want us to be fearful or anxious. As commanded in Philippians 4:6, we are not to let anxiety fill our soul. Anxiety is an enemy of God. An enemy of God is something that sets itself up against His plans, purposes, and will.

If anxiety is an enemy, however, then our anxiety cannot stand strong, sure, or firm when we praise God—because when we worship God, He sends an ambush against our enemies, as He did for the Judahites against the invaders.

Ultimately, anxiety is a response to a problem. Although the problem might be persistent, the anxiety we face isn't God's plan for our life. When we praise Him, lift up His name, and give thanks—even when it doesn't make sense—anxiety can't stay any longer.

Jesus advised His followers, "But the hour is coming, and is now here, when the true worshipers will worship the Father in spirit and in truth, for the father is seeking such people to worship him" (John 4:23). This true worship comes from a heart of truth. It must come from a heart that truly believes God is who He says He is and does what He says He does.

He can move in our life as He's moved in hundreds of peoples' lives before, and He can conquer our enemies. He can conquer our anxiety, fear, depression, and anything else that sets itself up against His plan.

This doesn't necessarily mean we will get our way in every situation, or that the problem will resolve in the precise way we wanted it to, but the fear associated with that problem or anxiety will be lifted.

Anxiety is never necessary, but it's overwhelmingly unnecessary in some of our lives. We give way too much attention and thought to our issues. However, when we worship, fix our trust and eyes on Jesus, and offer all we have to God, then what hold can anxiety have in your life anymore? When we let go of the anxiety, we might ask God to take it away, but must also relax our grip.

Some of us might cling to anxiety because, perversely, we feel better when we feel worse. We like the attention it gives us. We like people surrounding and comforting us—we like the pity party that comes with wallowing in our grief. We love anxiety sometimes.

But God knows better and wants us to let it go, because it's causing us trouble and pain. It's causing us to be separated from Him in some areas of our life, and He wants everything in us available to praise Him. And so we praise Him with open hands, offering our anxiety to Him.

When we worship God, it speaks the opposite language of anxiety, because anxiety speaks doom and death and fear—the language of the enemy. Anxiety has come to steal, kill, and destroy.

However, Jesus said He came to bring life in abundance (John 10:10). Therefore, when we worship and praise Him, anxiety can't stand strong. Praise dismantles the strongholds of anxiety in your life.

King Jehoshaphat and the Judahites learned this firsthand. Second Chronicles 20:24 continues, "When Judah came to the watchtower of the wilderness, they looked towards the horde, and behold, there were dead bodies lying on the ground, none had escaped."

When the warriors of Judah came to the place that overlooked the desert, where they expected to see a conquering host of enemies from three nations, they were astonished to find that the enemy had defeated itself. The Judahites didn't so much as have to lift a sword or loose an arrow. The battle truly was God's, just as He had promised—and the same is true for our battles.

Give Your Anxiety to God

Our anxiety cannot stand up to God, but we must surrender it to Him. We must discipline ourselves to wait until God gets there and resolves the situation, instead of trying to fight our anxiety out of our own strength. Be patient and let Him deal with it!

The enemy tries to bring us down with anxiety and fear. He tries to manipulate where we go, what we do, and what we say. He keeps us from living up to our potential by leading us to worry that we aren't good enough—that we have no potential.

Perhaps, then, we haven't lived up to the plans and purposes of God for our life because of some source of anxiety.

Maybe we think we could never accomplish something great because we don't have the training or education, or because we feel unworthy and ashamed before other people or before God. We make all kinds of excuses as the enemy fills our life with fear, trying to rob us of our inheritance, our joy, and our potential.

But today it stops, because we have the chance to say, "You know what? No longer will I let this keep happening. Anxiety, you have no hold over me anymore!" Then we need to start praising God, which brings His presence into our situations so that hell can shut up and stop speaking lies into our ears.

So this very instant, let's stop believing the falsehoods the enemy propagates about our worthlessness. Others may warn us that we will lose our job or be rendered obsolete, or that we won't be able to accomplish the goals that God has instilled in our heart. But it doesn't matter what messages we are hearing from others. Praise and give thanks, "for his steadfast love endures forever" (Psalm 136:1)!

Even when it doesn't make sense, we must learn to offer God praise. Then "the peace of God, which transcends all understanding"—that is, which is far greater than what we know or think could happen—"will guard your hearts and your minds in Christ Jesus" (Philippians 4:7 NIV). Then the anxiety, when denied access to us, will be vanquished. But it begins with praise.

When we praise, we remind the enemy that anything he has thrown our way—whatever he has done to try to steal from us, kill us, and destroy us—is ineffectual. "You know what, devil? I am still living. I am still breathing. And I am still praising! For Psalm 150:6 says, 'Let everything that has breath praise the LORD.'"

Let us continue praising God with everything we've got, until that dying day when we breathe our last breath. And even then, throughout all of eternity, we will praise our God and our King. It all comes down to praising Him!

I don't know what you're facing specifically in your life right now, but I know this: whatever you are facing isn't bigger than God. If you praise Him and usher His presence into your situation, then anxiety, fear and feelings of worthlessness, will diminish in the light of His glory.

Let's fully grasp these words and absorb them into our minds and hearts: "I will turn my head and fix my eyes on 'Jesus, the author and perfecter of our faith'" (Hebrews 12:2 NIV). The Lord Jesus brought us into existence, and He perfects us if we are found in Him.

That doesn't mean we ourselves are perfect, but it means He can cleanse us of all anxiety and sin and everything else that's not God's will. He can perfect our lives if we surrender it all to Him.

Therefore, let's begin by training our tongue, so that our first response to fear and anxiety will always be, "Praise my God and my King, whose love endures forever!"

WORKBOOK

Chapter 4 Questions

Question: What are three tools for stopping anxiety and fear? Give an example of how you could use one of these tools in the midst of a difficult circumstance you're experiencing today.

_____

_____

_____

_____

_____

_____

_____

_____

_____

_____

Question: What does it look like to train your tongue to praise?

_____

_____

_____

_____

_____

_____

_____

_____

_____

_____

_____

Question: What often gets in the way of you praising God? What steps can you take to clear the way for praise?

_____

_____

_____

_____

_____

_____

_____

_____

_____

_____

Question: How did King Jehoshaphat remember to believe in God? How can you remind yourself to believe in God this week?

_____
_____
_____
_____
_____
_____
_____
_____
_____
_____

Question: How does knowing the battle belongs to God comfort you? What would giving your anxiety to God look like?

_____
_____
_____
_____
_____
_____
_____
_____
_____
_____

Action: Spend some time worshiping God for who He is! Meditate on Psalm 22:3 and then write out a list of praises to God. Write out a prayer to God that reflects upon His power and asks for His help as you seek to overflow with a heart of thanksgiving in every circumstance.

Chapter 4 Notes

CHAPTER FIVE

Take Your Victory

In 1995, when I was in Grade 2, marbles were all the rage in school. Kids these days might not even know what marbles are, but I've always been partial to the cat's eye and galaxy patterns. I loved and collected marbles.

During this time, my dad went to Ireland to visit his family. While he was away, he bought some souvenirs. He returned with a collector's edition, king-sized galaxy marble, which was black with tiny speckles. Though I knew it probably only cost about ten cents, it was special because my dad had brought it back all the way from Ireland, and gave it to me.

I took all of my marbles to school because at recess and lunch my classmates and I would play. The day I brought my new galaxy marble to school, another boy and I decided to verse one another. We agreed to play for friendlies—that is, we would keep our own marbles regardless of who won—instead of for keeps.

Because we were playing for friendlies, I thought it was the perfect chance to bring out my awesome galaxy marble my dad got me.

So we played against each other. I flicked my marble out, and he flicked out his. I moved mine a little bit, and he rolled his, which hit mine. Then, before I could grab my marble, he grabbed both marbles.

I didn't understand what was happening. I told him I thought we were playing for friendlies, but he denied it: "No, that was keeps."

I protested, "No, we agreed first, that was my special marble!" And I cried.

Next, I ran to my teacher and explained how the other boy and I were playing and had agreed to friendlies at the start, but now he had my marble. Of course, he lied about it to the teacher as well, which made me angry.

Our teacher didn't know whom to believe, so she flipped a coin. I was distraught and cried again when the coin landed on the wrong side.

The next day when I went to school, I was still upset and refused to speak to the bully who had stolen my marble.

Little did I know that at lunchtime, my best friend, Matthew, went out with his bag of marbles and challenged the bully to a match for keeps, and the boy agreed. The boy used my marble, while Matt whipped out his little cat's eye marble—and quickly won my king-sized galaxy back.

Though I don't even know where that galaxy marble is now, in that moment I was elated. My prize marble was once again in my possession.

Stolen Dreams

If you've ever lost something you treasured, or had it stolen from you, you know how upsetting it can be.

When we battle with anxiety and fear on our own, without God, they rob us of our dreams. They deprive us of opportunities. Perhaps we don't apply for the job we want because we don't think we're good enough. Maybe we lose friends and miss out on exciting experiences because we're too afraid to leave the house and expose ourselves to other people.

Anxiety and fear are tools of the enemy of God, who comes to steal, kill, and destroy your life, but Jesus said, in effect, "I have come so you can experience abundant life" (see John 10:10). Some of us have been robbed by negative experiences, anxiety and fear that's come against our lives.

Some people have been overcome with anxiety in their battles. Some have experienced pain and loss for a long time because of the fear that fills their souls. No matter how badly they've wanted to get rid of it, it hasn't gone away.

Though the enemy has diminished our confidence, stifled our joy, and stolen our peace, our relationships, and our success, God wants to restore our strength to us. He doesn't want us to remain deprived or depressed, but to be whole, hopeful, and joyful.

Thus, once we've trapped our thoughts, turned our head to God, and trained our tongue to praise Him, it's time to take our victory.

Our God of Restoration

Though the enemy intends evil for us, God intends good for our situations. His plan for victory involves restoring and transforming our lives, regardless of the odds. After all, He is a God who loves comeback stories, as King Jehoshaphat and the nation of Judah learned well.

Recall that Jehoshaphat was filled with deep-rooted anxiety over the armies approaching Judah. But he trapped the thought by declaring praises and remembering what God had done in the past.

Then he turned his head toward God. God spoke to the Judahites and told them to face the enemy host, but not to fight, because He would fight the battle on their behalf.

As the Judahite army went forth to face the invaders, King Jehoshaphat led with the praise team. Although they didn't know the outcome, they sang and gave thanks to the Lord. Meanwhile, God ensured that the hostile armies fell prey to ambushes and destroyed each other in the confusion. The enemy was defeated.

Next, we find that the Judahites, as the victors, got to reap the spoils. When I first read this passage, I didn't know what 'spoils' were—I only knew that a spoiled person is a brat. However, spoils are essentially loot or other perks resulting from victory in war.

Second Chronicles explains how Jehoshaphat and Judah collected their spoils:

When Jehoshaphat and his people came to take their spoil, they found among them, in great numbers, goods, clothing, and precious things, which they took for themselves until they could carry no more. They were three days in taking the spoil, it was so much.

On the fourth day they assembled in the Valley of Beracah, for there they blessed the LORD. Therefore the name of that place has been called the Valley of Beracah to this day. Then they returned, every man of Judah and Jerusalem, and Jehoshaphat at their head, returning to Jerusalem with joy, for the LORD had made them rejoice over their enemies. They came to Jerusalem with harps and lyres and trumpets, to the house of the LORD. And the fear of God came on all the kingdoms of the countries when they heard that the LORD had fought against the enemies of Israel. So the realm of Jehoshaphat was quiet, for his God gave him rest all around. — 2 Chronicles 20:25–30

Notice in verse 25, the biblical narrative recounts, "They were there three days in taking the spoil, it was so much." How amazing God's blessing is! The Judahites thought they would be killed, but in the end, they didn't so much as have to pick up a weapon or fight—they simply gave it all to God and reaped the benefits.

When we take our hands off the steering wheel and say, "God, I believe You are in control of my life, and I trust You with all of it," we reap the rewards and blessings that follow.

For when we fix our eyes on Him—when we align ourselves with His plan for us, sit under Him and remain faithful, and claim the death and resurrection of Jesus in our lives—then from that moment, the resurrection power should be evident in us through restoration.

In short, we should be changed people as Christians. We shouldn't be living the same life and dealing with the same issues over and over again when we've got a God who steps in and makes a way where we saw none. God says in His Word that He is a God of restoration (Joel 2:25), and He wants to heal and restore us in our hearts and our circumstances, accordingly.

Another example of God's restoration in the Bible is the story of Joseph. Of twelve brothers, he was the second-youngest and his father's favourite. After sharing a dream that he would rule over his jealous brothers, they sold him to slavery, stained his special coat with blood, and lied to their father, telling him Joseph had died (Genesis 37).

Joseph became a slave in a palace, found himself blamed for something he didn't do, and went to jail. There God helped him interpret a dream of another prisoner, and later he interpreted a dream for the Pharaoh himself—who promptly promoted Joseph and placed him in charge of all land and food distribution in Egypt (Genesis 39–41).

Many years later, there was a famine, and Joseph's brothers travelled all the way to Egypt to purchase food. Though they were not expecting to see their brother in charge, Joseph saw them coming. Now he could get payback by jailing them, denying them food, or punishing them in some other manner (Genesis 42).

Joseph could have dwelled on his time in jail and how his hopes and dreams of being a leader among his brothers had been stolen. When he was in jail, it didn't seem the promise of being a great leader would come to pass.

Yet he remained faithful to God and kept his eyes fixed on Him. Joseph kept doing what God had called him to do, because he knew God restores.

And indeed, God blew Joseph's dreams away! I don't think Joseph ever imagined he would become a leader of an entire nation. But Joseph recognised God's restoration and blessing in the turn of events, saying to his brothers, "As for you, you meant evil against me but God meant it for good to bring it about that many people should be kept alive as they are today" (Genesis 50:20).

When we keep our eyes fixed on God and keep chasing after Him, He turns into good that which the enemy stole from us and was meant for harm. In effect, He turns the enemy's plans on their head—and the effects are often astonishing.

Our God of Blessing

We may feel like we don't deserve such blessing, recognising there are people with far greater problems than ours. But like Joseph, we must understand why God gives us the blessing He does—for His glory and for the good of all His people.

In the story of Jehoshaphat, 2 Chronicles 20:26 says that after the Judahites had spent three days collecting as much loot as they could carry, on the fourth day "they assembled in the Valley of Beracah, for there they blessed the LORD."

In the last chapter, we talked about how it's important to continue to praise God even when our problems still seem overwhelming or the situation doesn't make sense.

Our praise invites Him into the situation, ushering in his presence so He can take the lead. So we lift Him up and give thanks even in the midst of crisis.

But what's equally important, after danger or difficulty has passed, when His blessing is poured into our life, is that we continue to keep the language of praise going. In this way, we're establishing that we see God as more than a "get out of jail free" card. To the contrary, our offerings of praise in the wake of restoration help establish and maintain our eternal perspective regardless of our circumstances in the moment.

So we declare, "I believed You would do it, I declared it, and I praised You for it when it didn't make sense. And now that it's done, I still give You praise. I still say You are worthy—I still put You in that place of honour."

Thus, the people of Judah stopped reaping the spoils of victory on the fourth day so they could assemble together and worship God, blessing His name.

We, too, need to bless God, who blesses us. We need to lift His name high in the good and bad times alike—when He does what He says He will do, as well as when He doesn't do what we think He should do.

A Place of Blessing

Of the place where the Judahites gathered to praise God for the victory He'd won on their behalf, 2 Chronicles 20:26 notes, "Therefore the name of that place has been called the Valley of Beracah to this day."

According to the footnote in the English Standard Version of 2 Chronicles 20:26, 'Beracah' means "blessing." They called it the Valley of Blessing because after God had brought them out of a deadly situation, which had filled them with anxiety and dread, He had blessed them. They had collected the material spoils from the vanquished armies, and then they stopped and thanked God.

For our part, we as Christians must learn to stand and declare, "From now on, my life will be known as a valley of blessing. My life will be known as a life in which God accomplishes what He intends and promises. My life will be known as a life that gives God glory and honour in good times and bad. My life is a testimony to God—a valley of blessing."

We must also remember that God doesn't bless us only for our own sake. He doesn't want us to live in anxiety and fear, but nor does He intend for our lives to be rosy and sweet, without regard for others.

In the Western world especially, some of our churches give the impression of asking continuously for God's blessing without giving much thought to how we ought to use that blessing.

Certainly, we don't *deserve* God's blessing, and thus we are not blessed so we can keep it all to ourselves. Rather, we are blessed so we can be a blessing to others in turn.

Therefore, as God sets you free from fear and restores your hope and joy, let your restoration transform you into a conduit for blessing others in Jesus' name.

Chapter 5 Questions

Question: When have you been robbed of living an abundant life as a result of anxiety or fear? How, specifically, did your emotions deprive you of life as God intended? What kept you from victory?

_____

_____

_____

_____

_____

_____

_____

_____

_____

_____

Question: How do you reap reward from turning a situation over to God? What does this teach us about God's character?

_____

_____

_____

_____

_____

_____

_____

_____

_____

_____

_____

Question: How does training our heart to praise result in transformed thinking?

_____

_____

_____

_____

_____

_____

_____

_____

_____

_____

_____

Question: What does Joseph's life teach us about praise? How did Joseph bless others?

_____

_____

_____

_____

_____

_____

_____

_____

_____

_____

Question: Why should our restoration result in blessing others?

_____

_____

_____

_____

_____

_____

_____

_____

_____

_____

Action: Take the victory over anxiety and fear! Reflect on how God brings restoration in your life and throughout the stories you've read in the Bible. Read through the story of Joseph (Genesis 37:39–50), observing how he fixed his eyes on God repeatedly and how God restored him. Write down two ways you can use your restoration to bless others this week.

Chapter 5 Notes

CONCLUSION

Blessed to Be a Blessing

If you have food in your fridge, clothes to wear, a roof over your head, and at least a little money to spare in your bank account or wallet, you're wealthier than the vast majority of people in the world today.

Though similar sayings have become commonplace, appearing as quotations on inspirational posters and garnering countless social media 'likes,' they amount to a truly remarkable observation: most of us in developed nations enjoy immense material blessings relative to the rest of the world.

What are you doing with your blessing?

Remember, you are blessed to be a blessing. You are not blessed so you can have an easy, successful life. God doesn't want you to be just a successful person—He wants you to be a fruitful person. He wants you to have a ripple effect that consumes not only you but also the rest of your world.

When God frees you from fear and anxiety, and vanquishes the tangible as well as invisible threats that come

against you, ask yourself: "How am I a blessing to the people I encounter in my life?"

If you have been set free from anxiety and fear, God has turned it all around for you. He brought freedom, blessing, and life-change your way. He restored your dreams, opportunities, and relationships. But the moment He did so, He determined you would be a beacon of blessing and light that shines to the rest of your world and proclaims: He did it!

God Did It!

I love how the story of Jehoshaphat and the invading army ends—with peace in the kingdom and peace of mind:

> *And the fear of God came on all the kingdoms of the countries when they heard that the Lord had fought against the enemies of Israel. So the realm of Jehoshaphat was quiet, for his God gave him rest all around.* **— 2 Chronicles 20:29–30**

It's a beautiful ending to the story—"God gave him rest all around." We all love happy endings, don't we?

Our anxiety and fear set themselves up as enemies of God in their attempts to control our minds and hearts. The enemy employs anxiety so we won't realise God's power in our lives. He doesn't want us to realise that if God were in control, the perceived threats against us could soon be over and done with.

The enemy would much rather we remain intimidated and weighed down, nurturing and growing our fearful thoughts until they immobilise us.

But remember, victory and blessing aren't about me or you. We don't fight the battle—He fights for us. We don't attack and vanquish the source of danger, fear, and anxiety—we simply hand the matter over to Him.

We trap our thoughts, turn our head, and fix our eyes on Him, who holds our existence in His hands. As He protects us and provides for us in our trial, we train our tongue to speak praise in spite of the circumstances. Then we stand firm in victory when the enemy comes against us with worries and deceptions, because we know God has us covered.

I observe some Christians who walk with strength because they know the power of God in their lives. They're not alienated or anxious or disconnected. Rather, they're connected to God and to others in their relationship with Jesus. They have cultivated an eternal perspective of faith.

Likewise, each of us must understand the power of God in our lives and His power over the things that come against us. They can't destroy or conquer us, any more than the foreign hosts could conquer Jerusalem under Jehoshaphat. We must truly believe God is a God of blessing and restoration.

Today, release your anxiety and fear. Let it go, let God deal with it, and take your victory! Pick up the spoils of victory that anxiety and fear have left behind: the opportunities you've missed in the past, the friends you've lost, and the joy stolen from you. Pick up the confidence you haven't had for a long time. It's all lying there for you because Jesus has triumphed over the enemy, and God will defeat the enemy in your life as well.

As you take your victory, set your life up as a testimony to the greatness and blessing of God's goodness.

If someone asks you how you conquered anxiety and fear, or how you overcome an obstacle in your life, give God the credit and allow the other person to ride on your testimony of faith. Even if he or she doesn't believe in God, you can still share the fruits of your eternal perspective.

If we are faithful to do this, we will serve as beacons of blessing to the people in our lives—and to future generations—so they understand our victory is all about God. Like King Jehoshaphat, let's live in such a way that our descendants tell our story to remind each other of what God can accomplish when we rely on Him.

Let's be a blessing.

REFERENCES

Notes

1. Graham, Billy. "The Cure for Anxiety." *Billy Graham Evangelistic Association.* 9 July 2004. https://billygraham.org/decision-magazine/july-2004/the-cure-for-anxiety/
2. "Yir'ah." *NAS Old Testament Hebrew Lexicon.* In *Bible Study Tools.* http://www.biblestudytools.com/lexicons/hebrew/nas/yirah.html
3. Milne, A. A. "In Which Piglet Does a Very Grand Thing." In *The House at Pooh Corner.* Methuen, 1928.
4. Goodman, Brenda. "Even Mild Anxiety May Shorten a Person's Life." Reviewed by Louise Chang, MD. *WebMD.* http://www.webmd.com/mental-health/news/20120731/mild-anxiety-may-shorten-persons-life#1

5. Swift, Taylor. "Shake It Off." Lyrics by Taylor Swift, Max Martin, & Shellback. *1989*. Big Machine, 2014.

6. Bethel Music. "It Is Well." *You Make Me Brave: Live at the Civic*. Bethel Music, 2014.

7. Ten Boom, Corrie. *The Hiding Place*. Chosen Books, 1971.

About the Author

Aaron and his wife, Jacqui, are the lead pastors of Fresh
Church, Melbourne, Australia. They live with their sons
Chris and Judah. Aaron loves Jesus, loves the church,
loves people, and loves life! He is full of energy,
strategic insight, creativity, and passion, and desires to
see people overcoming anxiety and fear in their lives and
encountering a fresh start in Jesus' name.

About Sermon To Book

SermonToBook.com began with a simple belief: that sermons should be touching lives, *not* collecting dust. That's why we turn sermons into high-quality books that are accessible to people all over the globe.

Turning your sermon series into a book exposes more people to God's Word, better equips you for counselling, accelerates future sermon prep, adds credibility to your ministry, and even helps make ends meet during tight times.

John 21:25 tells us that the world itself couldn't contain the books that would be written about the work of Jesus Christ. Our mission is to try anyway. Because in heaven, there will no longer be a need for sermons or books. Our time is now.

If God so leads you, we'd love to work with you on your sermon or sermon series.

Visit www.sermontobook.com to learn more.

www.ingramcontent.com/pod-product-compliance
Lightning Source LLC
LaVergne TN
LVHW052033080426
835513LV00018B/2300